For Dad—B.W.
For Jacob—A.G.

ACKNOWLEDGMENTS

Thank-you to Bruce Markusen, author of several books on baseball and currently a teacher at the National Baseball Hall of Fame and Museum, the Farmer's Museum, and the Fenimore Art Museum, and to Meryl C. S. Troop, Interpreter/Civil Rights Advocate, staff, and friends at the Maine Center on Deafness for reviewing this story and for their valuable input.

AUTHOR'S NOTE

One of the original meanings of the word *dumb* was "lacking the power of speech," and during the time William Hoy lived (1860s–1960s), the word was used to refer to a person who did not speak. The nickname Dummy was sometimes given to such a person. Today, using *dumb* this way is derogatory, and the nickname is offensive to those who are deaf. *Deaf* is the term of identity that is embraced by the community of deaf people who communicate with sign language.

AUTHOR'S SOURCES

Berger, Ralph. "William Hoy." The Baseball Biography Project/Society for American Baseball Research (SABR). http://bioproj.sabr.org/bioproj.cfm?a=v&bid=832&pid=0.

Chase, Dennis. "Hoy, William Ellsworth 'Dummy'." *Biographical Dictionary of American Sports: Baseball*. David L. Porter, ed. Westport, CT: Greenwood Press, 2000.

"Dummy" Hoy Homeplate. MSM Productions, Ltd. http://www.dummyhoy.com.

Gould, Stephen Jay. *Triumph and Tragedy in Mudville: A Lifelong Passion for Baseball*. New York: W. W. Norton & Co., 2004.

Ritter, Lawrence S. *The Glory of Their Times: The Story of the Early Days of Baseball Told by the Men Who Played It*. New York: Macmillan, 1966.

p. 29: "I'm glad . . . you!" Quoted in Ralph Berger, "William Hoy." The Baseball Biography Project/Society for American Baseball Research (SABR).

Text copyright © 2012 by Bill Wise
Illustrations copyright © 2012 by Adam Gustavson
All rights reserved. No part of this book may be reproduced, transmitted, or stored in an information retrieval system in any form or by any means, electronic, mechanical, photocopying, recording, or otherwise, without written permission from the publisher.
LEE & LOW BOOKS Inc., 95 Madison Avenue, New York, NY 10016
leeandlow.com
Manufactured in China by Toppan, February 2012
Book design by Scott Myles Studios
Book production by The Kids at Our House
The text is set in Dutch 801
The illustrations are rendered in oil on paper
10 9 8 7 6 5 4 3 2 1
First Edition
Library of Congress Cataloging-in-Publication Data
Wise, Bill.
Silent star : the story of deaf major leaguer William Hoy / by Bill Wise ; pictures by Adam Gustavson.
p. cm.
Summary: "A biography of William 'Dummy' Hoy, who pursued his love of baseball and became the first deaf player to have a long career in the Major Leagues, where he accumulated records and top-ranking statistics. Includes an afterword, author's sources, and historical photograph"—Provided by publisher.
ISBN 978-1-60060-411-9 (hardcover : alk. paper)
1. Hoy, William, 1862-1961. 2. Baseball players—United States—Biography. 3. Deaf athletes—United States—Biography.
I. Gustavson, Adam, ill. II. Title.
GV865.H685 2011
796.357092—dc23   [B]   2011036827

SILENT STAR

THE STORY OF DEAF MAJOR LEAGUER WILLIAM HOY

BY
BILL WISE

PICTURES BY
ADAM GUSTAVSON

LEE & LOW BOOKS INC. • NEW YORK

June 19, 1889. From his center field position, Washington Nationals star William Hoy eyed the opposing team's base runner stretching his lead off second base, eager to score. Hoy had already thrown out two runners at home plate earlier in the game. Would this base runner also challenge Hoy's arm?

Hoy peered in at the pitcher's mound. The Nationals pitcher was exhausted. His fastball had lost its zip, and Hoy knew it. With his pitcher tiring and a left-handed batter at the plate, Hoy decided to move closer to right field.

The pitcher released the ball. The batter swung and blasted a scorching single toward Hoy. The base runner was off with the crack of the bat. Hoy, realizing there was going to be a play at home plate, charged the hard-hit ball. He snagged it cleanly on the second bounce and came up firing. The ball shot out of Hoy's hand like a cannonball and whistled its way to the catcher at home plate. The base runner slid wide of the plate in hopes of avoiding the tag, but the Nationals catcher swept his mitt across the diving runner.

"He's out!" shouted the umpire through the cloud of dust.

With his game-saving play, Hoy had made history. He became the first player ever to throw out three runners at home plate in one game!

The crowd erupted into cheers. Then the fans did something else, something they always did to show their appreciation when Hoy made a great play. They threw confetti up in the air and wildly waved their arms and hats and handkerchiefs.

The fans made such a visual commotion because William Hoy was deaf.

William Ellsworth Hoy was not born deaf. When he was three years old, he became very sick. He developed a high fever and chills, and was too weak to get out of bed. With each day William was ill, his family grew more worried. Finally a doctor came to the Hoys' farm in rural Houcktown, Ohio. He told William's parents that their son had a serious infection called meningitis. The doctor shook his head sadly and said that there was nothing he could do to help the little boy.

William was sick for many more days. Then, at last, he began to get better. His family was relieved, but they soon found out that something had changed. The illness had left William deaf. He could not hear well enough to understand speech.

As a young child in the 1860s, William struggled with his deafness. Because he could not hear, his speaking skills were very limited. He often used a pencil and paper to write down what he wanted to say.

Some children teased William or were afraid to play with him because he was deaf and did not use his voice to communicate. Adults could be thoughtless too, looking down on the boy or ignoring him altogether. Friendly and personable, William was confused, his feelings hurt. Everyone was different in some way. He wondered why people could not accept him as he was.

When William was ten years old, his parents sent him to the Ohio School for the Deaf in Columbus. William loved the school. For the first time in his life he felt that he fit in. Nobody stared or pointed at him. Nobody felt sorry for him.

William learned to use American Sign Language and to read lips. He enjoyed his classes in reading, writing, and mathematics. His absolute favorite thing, though, was the school baseball team. William had played ball with his brothers back home, but that was nothing like this. The school team had real uniforms, real umpires, real games.

Every night William dreamed of playing major league baseball, but making his dream come true was a real long shot. There had been only two deaf players—both pitchers—in the big leagues. At the time, a pitcher played about once every four days. William was an outfielder, a position that was played every day. No deaf everyday-position player had ever reached the major leagues.

After William graduated from high school in 1879, he wondered what he would do next. Not many jobs were open to deaf people. So William's father convinced him to learn shoemaking, a trade that many deaf men entered.

Back in Houcktown, at the age of eighteen, William went to work as an apprentice in the local shoemaker's shop. There William was taught everything about fixing and making shoes. Day after day, he sat on a wooden bench, toiling in the back of the store. All the work was done by hand, a slow and tedious process. Even though William would have preferred to be playing baseball, he worked diligently. He took pride in everything he did.

Soon William had saved enough money to buy the shoemaker's shop. When the sale was completed, one of the first things William did was build a baseball diamond on the weedy plot of land out back. Then he invited the local teenagers to play ball there.

For most of the year, work kept William so busy, he had no time for baseball. But during the summer, when many townspeople went barefoot, the shoe business was slow. Sometimes William would temporarily close the shop and join the backyard games.

One June day in 1885, a coach for an amateur baseball team passed through Houcktown. Always looking for new players, he stopped to watch the game behind the shoemaker's shop. The coach marveled at William's baseball skills.

After the game the coach approached, hoping to talk to this impressive player. He tapped William on the back and asked if he would like to play baseball for an amateur team.

William turned around. He had no idea what the coach had just said. To show the man that he was deaf, William began speaking in sign language.

Unnerved by the rapid hand movements, the coach abruptly took off, leaving William bewildered.

The next day, however, the coach returned. Once again William dazzled him. And once again the coach approached after the game. This time the coach was prepared. He reached into his shirt pocket, pulled out a pencil and a notepad, and wrote out an offer for William Hoy to play on his team. Delighted, Hoy nodded and shook the coach's hand. For the rest of the summer, Hoy traveled to towns and cities around Ohio playing games with his new team.

A year later, Hoy tried out for the Oshkosh club, a minor league baseball team. Most folks were sure Hoy would get cut. A deaf player at the amateur level was one thing. But they doubted he could make it playing with the pros.

Hoy proved them wrong. He played so well, he was offered a spot on the Oshkosh team. Leaving the shoe business behind, he closed the shop for good and joined the minor leagues.

Minor league baseball was full of professional players who would do anything to gain an advantage. Because he could not hear the home plate umpire shouting balls and strikes when he was at bat, Hoy had to turn around to look at the ump after each pitch. The umpire would repeat the call, and as Hoy read the ump's lips, opposing pitchers often quick pitched Hoy, throwing the next ball before he was ready to bat. As a result, Hoy's hitting suffered, and he struggled at the plate. He finished the season with a dismal .219 batting average.

Hoy did not give up on his dream. Between seasons he came up with a plan that allowed him to follow the home plate umpire's calls. When he returned to Oshkosh for the 1887 season, Hoy was ready. His plan was simple. After each pitch, he would glance down the left field line at his team's third base coach. The coach would thrust his left arm in the air to indicate that the ump had called a ball, his right arm in the air if the ump had called a strike. Hoy no longer had to turn around. He was always ready for the next pitch.

That season Hoy batted .368, one of the best batting averages in minor league baseball. His performance did not go unnoticed. Shortly after the season ended, he received an invitation to try out for the Washington Nationals of the National League.

The news that William Hoy had been contacted by a major league team traveled quickly throughout Ohio. Again, most people thought he would fail. They believed big league baseball was no place for a man who could not hear or talk.

It did not matter to Hoy what people thought. He knew he would succeed. He was determined to prove to everyone that a deaf person could indeed play major league baseball. And if he could make it, maybe other deaf players could make it too.

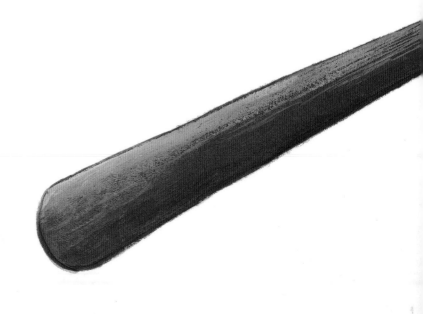

Competition in training camp was tough. Hoy had to battle good players from all over the country. But Hoy worked hard. He paid close attention to the other players and anticipated all the possible plays on the bases and in the field. By the end of camp, Hoy had earned a starting position on the Nationals.

Years ago the word *dumb* was used to mean "not able to speak," and Hoy's new teammates quickly tagged him with the nickname Dummy. Today calling a deaf person dumb would be derogatory and offensive, but in Hoy's day it was acceptable. Hoy carried his nickname with pride. Dummy became the name he preferred, and he often corrected people who called him William.

Over the next fourteen years, Hoy left no doubt in anyone's mind that he was one of baseball's best and smartest players. Season after season, he consistently ranked among major league leaders in assists, putouts, walks, singles, stolen bases, and times on base. Sportswriters called him the best fielding outfielder in the National League.

In the spring of 1900, another deaf player signed a major league contract. Luther Taylor, a Kansas farm boy, joined the New York Giants as a starting pitcher. Hoy thought it would be an honor to bat against Taylor one day. Two years later, when Hoy was playing for the Cincinnati Reds, he had that opportunity.

On May 16, 1902, Hoy's team hosted Taylor's New York Giants. For the first—and only—time ever, a deaf batter would face a deaf pitcher in a big league game. Thousands of fans crammed the Cincinnati Reds beautiful new Palace of the Fans ballpark.

With a superb sinker ball, Taylor had quickly established himself as a top-notch pitcher. Hoy knew that Taylor was the opposition while on the playing field, but he also admired the young pitcher. As Hoy approached home plate to bat, he politely greeted Taylor. "I'm glad to see you!" Hoy signed.

Hoy took his stance in the batter's box.

Taylor went into his windup and unleashed his trademark sinker. The ball started out high and then dropped sharply into the strike zone. Hoy stood his ground, but did not swing.

Strike one!

Hoy dug in for the next pitch. Taylor reared back and threw another sinker. This time Hoy swung—and missed.

Strike two!

Hoy stepped out of the batter's box and rapped the sides of his cleats with his bat. Stepping back to the plate, he moved to the front of the box.

Taylor wound up and fired a pitch headed for the lower outside corner of the plate. Hoy was ready. He pounded a ground ball that scooted past the shortstop and into center field for a base hit.

As Hoy stood on first base, he exhaled. Then he looked at Taylor. The young pitcher gave Hoy a slight tip of his hat. Hoy tipped his hat too, and smiled.

Taylor and the New York Giants won the game that day. The Cincinnati Reds did not like to lose, but Hoy could not help but feel proud. Two deaf players had squared off against each other in a major league game. It was an historic day for baseball.

A year later, in 1903, Hoy retired from professional baseball. He bought a sixty-acre farm near Cincinnati, where he and his wife, Anna, who was also deaf, raised their three children. Hoy proved to be as skillful at farming as he was at playing baseball. He operated a successful dairy business for more than twenty years.

In 1924 Hoy sold the farm and became a personnel director for several hundred deaf employees at the Goodyear Rubber Company in Akron, Ohio. He also coached and umpired in deaf baseball leagues.

Hoy remained connected to professional baseball too. Because of his contributions to the sport, he was awarded a lifetime pass to major league baseball events. He attended games right up until his death at the age of ninety-nine.

William "Dummy" Hoy was an inspiration to all who met him. Never giving up on his dream, he overcame numerous obstacles to become the first deaf player to have a long and distinguished career in the major leagues. He was a courageous, determined hero.

★ AFTERWORD ★

Of the tens of thousands of players who have made their careers in major league baseball, William Ellsworth "Dummy" Hoy (1862–1961) ranks in the top twenty-five in the following all-time career statistics: stolen bases, assists by an outfielder, and double plays by an outfielder. As of 2012, he remains one of only three outfielders to record three assists to home plate in one game and is the only outfielder ever to lead a major league in assists, putouts, and fielding percentage in the same season. Hoy threw right-handed and batted left-handed. He scored 100 runs or more in a single season nine times, stole 30 or more bases in a season eleven times, and registered more than 2,000 career hits. These statistics are impressive when compared with those of many of baseball's all-time greatest players.

Some baseball historians credit Hoy with influencing the use of hand signals by umpires. Hoy's involvement began when he played on the Oshkosh team and developed a method for following the home plate umpire's calls. Other historians contend that umpires began using hand signals several years after Hoy left the game.

In 1951, Hoy was among the first people entered into the American Athletic Association of the Deaf's Hall of Fame. He was inducted into the Ohio Baseball Hall of Fame in 1992, and the Cincinnati Reds Hall of Fame in 2003. In addition to Luther Taylor's success, Hoy's opened the door for other deaf major league players, among them William Deegan, Dick Sipek, and Curtis Pride.

HOY, C. F., Washington

Library of Congress, Prints & Photographs Division
[LC-DIG-bbc-0383f]

Given Hoy's numerous accomplishments, several of his peers—including Hall of Famers Honus Wagner, Connie Mack, and Clark Griffith—said he deserved to be enshrined in the National Baseball Hall of Fame. People today are still advocating for Hoy to be inducted into the Hall of Fame, thereby giving full official recognition to his achievements.

"His record was remarkable. In black and white, it stands with the best of all time." —Pat Harmon, *The Sporting News*, December 27, 1961